MW01592446

Christian
Encouragement

Exhorting Believers to
Encourage the Brethren

Copyrighted Material

Copyright © 2018 by Paul M. Kadow

Also known as Mike Kadow

The author may be contacted:

Email: pmkadow@gmail.com

Scripture quotations are from the ESV© Bible (The Holy Bible, English Standard Version®), copyright ©2001 by Crossway, a publishing ministry of Good News Publishers. Used by permission. All rights reserved.

ISBN-9781724026903

Preface

> "Take care, brothers, lest there be in any of you an evil, unbelieving heart, leading you to fall away from the living God. But exhort one another every day, as long as it is called "today," that none of you may be hardened by the deceitfulness of sin. Hebrews 3:12,13. ESV

This booklet is written for those who want to learn how to become a better encourager. Encouragement is absolutely essential for a thriving Church. If a Church is going to flourish and not just exist, every member of the Church needs to be an encourager.

We all need encouragement, from the strongest Christian to the one just born again. It is so very easy to become discouraged and fall into the pit of discouragement. Where does discouragement lead? It leads to sin, which slowly hardens the heart by its deceitfulness. From Hebrews 3:13 quoted above.

Encouragement works with every gift of the Holy Spirit—those who have the gift of pastor, preacher, teacher, leader, evangelist, faith, fellowship, giving, mercy, and serving. Encouragement weaves itself in and through all these gifts, especially the greatest of them all, Love. See I Corinthians 13.

In this booklet, we will delve into the meaning and applications of encouragement.

In Amazon.com, search for:

"Christian Encouragement" – including the quotes

Dedication

I dedicate this booklet to my home church, Berean Presbyterian Church (PCA) of Ellwood City, PA. And to its Pastor, Elders, Deacons and the entire congregation. I have never known a church home like this one.

I am truly blessed!

Mike Kadow (Paul M. Kadow)

Email: pmkadow@gmail.com

Special thanks to my editor: Betty Banaszak

Edited by Betty Banaszak, author of *The Divided Kingdom* and its sequel *The Return from Babylon to Jerusalem* covering the kings and prophets from Solomon to Malachi. Available through Amazon.com.

I appreciate small books that get to the point quickly. As such, I am writing this short booklet on Christian Encouragement.

Table of Contents

Table of Contents

Table of Contents

Table of Contents

Chapter 1 Introduction

Where do we start?

We start with prayer.

> May the God of endurance and encouragement grant you to live in such harmony with one another, in accord with Christ Jesus, that together you may with one voice glorify the God and Father of our Lord Jesus Christ.
> Romans 15:5-6

What is encouragement?

From the dictionary: "the act of giving someone support, confidence, hope or the persuasion to do or continue doing something."

Another aspect of encouragement is to introduce a person to the grace of God that is available to them.

A third aspect of encouragement is one Christian greeting another with Christian charity. You will know you have been involved in this type of encouragement when you walk away feeling good about the grace of God operating in your life.

Encouragement always involves Philippians 2:3-4

> Do nothing from selfish ambition or conceit, but in humility count others more significant than yourselves. Let each of you look not only to his own interests, but also to the interests of others.
> Philippians 2:3-4

Encouragement is never selfish.

What is encouragement? I am not sure it can be defined exactly. It is more of an attitude, a feeling, a reaching out through the grace of God to other Christians for their benefit and the glory of God.

Encouraging a fellow believer

When you encourage a fellow believer, you are inflating the courage they have inside them, not like inflating a balloon with air, but inflating with something real, something of substance, the actual Word of God.

> As Jesus said:
> But he answered, "It is written,
> " 'Man shall not live by bread alone but by every word that
> comes from the mouth of God.' "
> Matthew 4:4

As you quote passages from the Bible that directly apply to a person's life, you are encouraging them.

Quoting I Corinthians 10:13 may help someone struggling with sin.

> No temptation has overtaken you that is not common to man.
> God is faithful, and he will not let you be tempted beyond
> your ability, but with the temptation he will also provide
> the way of escape, that you may be able to endure it.
> I Corinthians 10:13

Simple ways to encourage

Just recognizing a person, calling them by name when they enter a room, saying "Hi John," or "Hi Jane." Just recognizing a person encourages them.

Noticing something about them and commenting on it can also encourage.

You may say: "Nice shirt," or "Nice dress,"

Or "what a unique sweater";

Or you can simply say, "It is really nice to see you."

Always be on the lookout for something nice to compliment a person on.

But your praise must be genuine, it must not be phony. A phony encouragement is obvious immediately. Ignoring a person may tend to discourage them.

Why people need encouragement

We are people who are easily discouraged. Being a
Christian or not, we are easily discouraged.

Without encouragement, we are more likely to sin. Sin
is deceitful, and sin hardens us.

> Take care, brothers, lest there be in any of you an evil,
> unbelieving heart, leading you to fall away from the
> living God.
> But exhort one another every day,
> as long as it is called "today,"
> that none of you may be hardened
> by the deceitfulness of sin.
> Hebrews 3:12,13

Don't neglect meeting together

How can you be an encourager if you don't meet with
others?

> Not neglecting to meet together,
> as is the habit of some,
> but encouraging one another,
> and all the more as you see the
> Day drawing near.
> Hebrews 10:25

Being by yourself for long periods of time may tend
to be discouraging. There is no such thing as a "Lone
Ranger" Christian.

The practical side

Types of encouragement

- Face to Face, handshake to handshake, hug to hug (for the huggers that is)
- Notes, cards, letters, emails, texting, anything to show the person that you are thinking about them
- Meeting together on a regular basis

Common phrases to encourage

- Welcome!
- I like that!
- I am glad you are with us!
- I look forward to seeing you again.
- Now that is encouraging, thank you.
- Interesting way you put that.
- Good point!
- Nice verse you quoted, did you memorize it?
- Nice shirt, dress, etc.

  Be authentic and mean what you say, phonies are spotted right away. Be careful that you don't use the same phrase with more than one person.

A question to consider

- Can an introvert be an encourager?

  God made introverts as well as extroverts, so an introvert can and must be an encourager. But an introvert may encourage in different ways and may need to be more creative in thinking of ways to encourage.

Goals of encouragement

- Encourage a person to stay away from sin,
- Encourage the downhearted, one who may be suffering from depression,
- Encourage a person to do better,
- Encouragement must be genuine, not phony or forced,
- It is difficult to encourage if you do not take a real interest in the person.

What encouragement is not

- Don't encourage to be aggressive
- Don't encourage to cause pain
- Don't encourage to be confrontational
- Don't encourage to attack others

Chapter 2 Encouragement with Other Spiritual Gifts

Gifts from the Holy Spirit

As with other gifts of the Holy Spirit, encouragement does not stand alone. God created these gifts to work together, they are most effective in this way. Just as in any church or small group, it takes multiple gifts and multiple brethren to work for God's glory.

This chapter explores some of the ways that encouragement works with other gifts.

Romans 12 gives a list of many gifts of God's Holy Spirit.

> For by the grace given to me I say to everyone among you not to think of himself more highly than he ought to think, but to think with sober judgment, each according to the measure of faith that God has assigned. For as in one body we have many members, and the members do not all have the same function, so we, though many, are one body in Christ, and individually members one of another. Having gifts that differ according to the grace given to us, let us use them: if prophecy, in proportion to our faith; if service, in our serving; the one who teaches, in his teaching; the one who exhorts, in his exhortation; the one who contributes, in generosity; the one who leads, with zeal; the one who does acts of mercy, with cheerfulness.
> Romans 12:3-8

There are 3 other passages that talk about the gifts of the Spirit, no one passage lists them all. The Romans

12 passage is the one that most directly talks about encouragement.

Primary means of encouragement

Primarily the means of encouragement is to remind the hearer of the powerful and amazing work of God in Christ, particularly in regard to the saving work of Jesus in the atonement, in other words, salvation.

Preaching and encouragement

Preaching does not happen in a vacuum. The Holy Spirit of God must be present in the preacher, in the message, and in the hearer to be completely effective.

The same can be said for encouragement among Christians, it does not happen in a vacuum. The Holy Spirit of God must be present in the encourager, in the exhortation, and in the receiver to be completely effective.

After the service encouragement is at work between the hearers as they exhort, challenge and strengthen each other.

Good questions to ask fellow believers after a service are:

- What do you think of the message?
- What do you think of such and such point?
- Did you get that verse the pastor was referring to?
- Did you understand that point?

- What did the pastor mean when he said . . . ?
- Do you think the message was an encouragement?

Christ-centered fellowship & encouragement

When two or more believers are gathered together in His Name, another is present, the Holy Spirit. This is based on the promise from the Word of God.

> For where two or three are gathered in my name, there am I among them."
> Matthew 18:20

Each believer has the Holy Spirit inside of them (I Corinthians 6:19). From the promise of Matthew 18:20 the Holy Spirit is in their midst as well. So it is like having a double portion of the Holy Spirit, that is, the Holy Spirit dwelling inside of the believer and indwelling in their midst. This combination is encouraging indeed.

Adding faith into the mix

Based on faith, let us go a step further.

> So, faith comes from hearing,
> and hearing through the word of Christ.
> Romans 10:17

As we hear the word of God, faith is being infused into us. We have the blessing of faith being added to our current blessing of the Spirit dwelling inside of us, as well as in our midst. That is what I call encouragement!

His name

One last point, Matthew 18:20 says, "in my name." It may not work as effectively if a group of Christians is gathered solely for a social event. They need to be gathered around the name of Christ and the word of God.

Mutually encouraged by each other's faith

Faith may be a difficult item to quantify in a believer's life.

Consider the definition of faith from the book of Hebrews:

> Now faith is the assurance of things hoped for,
> the conviction of things not seen.
> Hebrews 11:1

Faith is a gift of the Holy Spirit, but faith can be fragile and may be easily diminished.

For most of us, our faith needs lots of encouragement.

Consider the passage below:

> First, I thank my God through Jesus Christ for all of you,
> because your faith is proclaimed in all the world.
> For God is my witness, whom I serve with
> my spirit in the gospel of his Son,
> that without ceasing I mention you always in my prayers,
> asking that somehow by God's will
> I may now at last succeed in coming to you.
> For I long to see you, that I may impart to you
> some spiritual gift to strengthen you,
> that is, that we may be mutually encouraged
> by each other's faith, both yours and mine.
> Romans 1:8-12

As you can see from the previous passage, we are mutually encouraged by each other's faith, and it is absolutely essential that Christians get together around Christ and His Word on a regular basis.

Humility

You cannot be an effective encourager if you are not humble and thinking about those whom you wish to encourage.

> Complete my joy by being of the same mind, having the same love, being in full accord and of one mind.
> Do nothing from selfish ambition or conceit, but in humility count others more significant than yourselves.
> Let each of you look not only to his own interests, but also to the interests of others.
> Philippians 2:2-4

From this passage, an encourager must be invested in the ones being encouraged. Think of those you consider encouragers when you meet them, who are they talking about? You, of course. I have seldom met a self-centered encourager.

Service

Service encompasses a whole range of activities.
Those with the gift of Service are always involved in
helping others. As in the Philippians 2 passage above,
everything is about others. This ties in directly with
encouragement. When another person is helping you,
are you not encouraged? In the same way, as you help
others, you are encouraged as well. From Isaiah 58:10:

> . . . if you pour yourself out for the hungry
> and satisfy the desire of the afflicted,
> then shall your light rise in the darkness
> and your gloom be as the noonday.
> Isaiah 58:10

Teaching

Teaching is a close cousin to preaching. Both impart
knowledge and application. Teaching may be a bit
more low-key, however. Think of the best teachers
you have had. Every one of them invested their lives
in you. And the result is that you are encouraged and
ready to take on bigger challenges.

A teacher focuses on the meaning and content of the
Word, an encourager focuses more on the practical
application of the Word.

Both a teacher and an encourager can relate to others
with understanding, sympathy, and positive guidance.

A teacher says, "This is the way you should go."

Encourager comes alongside you and says, "I will help you go that way."

The teacher needs to be wise and with that wisdom encourage ones to turn away from trouble.

> The teaching of the wise is a fountain of life,
> that one may turn away from the snares of death.
> Proverbs 13:14

And teach what is right.

> teaching them to observe all that I have commanded
> you. . . ."
> Matthew 28:20

Leadership

A leader must encourage others to follow. They need to inspire and encourage their followers. Encouragement is an integral part of leadership; true leadership, however, needs many other elements.

There are so many good leaders in the Bible, and a number of bad ones also.

Love and encouragement

It can be said that love is the greatest gift of them all. And God gives love to every Christian. Love is one of the strongest avenues of encouragement. How can you love a person without encouraging them to one degree or another? And if courage is stored in the human heart, how much more is love? Can you imagine love without encouragement, or encouragement without love?

> Love bears all things,
> believes all things,
> hopes all things,
> endures all things.
> I Corinthians 13:7

Chapter 3 Why Is Encouragement Important?

Without encouragement, sin

We are commanded to exhort each other every day.

Why? So that we are not hardened by the deceitfulness of sin.

Sin is extremely deceitful and may blind the eyes of your mind in less than a day if given a chance.

> "Take care, brothers, lest there be in any of you an evil, unbelieving heart, leading you to fall away from the living God. But exhort one another every day, as long as it is called "today," that none of you may be hardened by the deceitfulness of sin. Hebrews 3:12,13

Sin sneaks into our lives in many ways.

It always seems to start with something simple.

After the first little innocent sin, and nothing happens, we may think "that was not so bad." A few days later and there is another, and it continues. Your daily time with God becomes a little awkward, but He understands. Soon our time with God becomes less and less because it is not as full or meaningful. You are being hardened by the deceitfulness of sin.

Little sins are like threads, easily broken, so what is the harm, I can always break the habit, or so we think.

Slave to sin

Sin by sin by sin – thread by thread by thread and soon you have enough thread wrapped around you that you will be unable to move, at that point you are a slave to your sin. You may not know it because sin is blinding and deceitful. Or worse yet, you do know it, but don't care.

Consider what Jesus said in John 8:34:

> Jesus answered them,
> "Truly, truly, I say to you,
> everyone who practices sin is a slave to sin.
> John 8:34

Sins, simple sins, repeated again and again and therein lies sins deceitfulness, and you, my friend, are a slave to sin.

Do you practice sin? Or perhaps just a simple sin? Then you are a slave to sin.

Solomon from the Old Testament, the wisest man who ever lived, said it this way:

> The iniquities of the wicked ensnare him,
> and he is held fast in the cords of his sin.
> He dies for lack of discipline,
> and because of his great folly he is led astray.
> Proverbs 5:22-23

Hardened by the deceitfulness of sin

Let us consider the phrase "hardened by the deceitfulness of sin." Sin is indeed deceitful. Now when we combine the deceitfulness of sin with the deceitfulness of our own heart (Jeremiah 17:9), we may find ourselves really behind the eight ball Having our own sin being deceitful, and our own heart being deceitful, we all need encouragement badly.

Taken a step further, our desires may be deceitful also.

> You were taught, with regard to your former way of life, to put off your old self, which is being **corrupted by its deceitful desires;** to be made new in the attitude of your minds; Ephesians 4:22

Hardened

Before we leave this verse, please reflect on the word "hardened." Do we know when we are being hardened?

Is it obvious to us? How is it obvious?

Did the Egyptian Pharaoh back in Exodus know he was hardened through all 10 plagues? Read Exodus 7 through Exodus 12 for the story of this Pharaoh.

Discouragement

In the following passage, David is obviously discouraged. Being discouraged he cries out to the Lord. Notice one of the results of discouragement, "my spirit faints within me." He knows that there is no one who takes notice of him. He says, "no one cares for my soul." He is in a bad way.

> With my voice I cry out to the LORD;
> with my voice I plead for mercy to the LORD.
> I pour out my complaint before him;
> I tell my trouble before him.
> When my spirit faints within me,
> you know my way!
> In the path where I walk
> they have hidden a trap for me.
> Look to the right and see:
> there is none who takes notice of me;
> no refuge remains to me;
> no one cares for my soul.
> Psalm 142:1-4

Sin may cause discouragement

Psalm 38 is another passage where David is discouraged, but for another reason, his sin. Yes, sin does cause discouragement and even may even cause problems with physical health.

The answer to this discouragement? Repentance.

Psalm 38

O Lord, rebuke me not in your anger,
nor discipline me in your wrath!
For your arrows have sunk into me,
and your hand has come down on me.
There is no soundness in my flesh because of your
indignation;
there is no health in my bones because of my sin.
For my iniquities have gone over my head;
like a heavy burden, they are too heavy for me.
My wounds stink and fester because of my foolishness,
I am utterly bowed down and prostrate;
all the day I go about mourning.
For my sides are filled with burning,
and there is no soundness in my flesh.
I am feeble and crushed;
I groan because of the tumult of my heart.
O Lord, all my longing is before you;
my sighing is not hidden from you.
My heart throbs; my strength fails me,
and the light of my eyes—it also has gone from me.
My friends and companions stand aloof from my plague,
and my nearest kin stand far off.
Those who seek my life lay their snares;
those who seek my hurt speak of ruin
and meditate treachery all day long.
But I am like a deaf man; I do not hear,
like a mute man who does not open his mouth.

Psalm 38 continued on the next page.

Psalm 38 continued from the previous page.

> I have become like a man who does not hear,
> and in whose mouth are no rebukes.
> But for you, O Lord, do I wait;
> it is you, O Lord my God, who will answer.
> For I said, "Only let them not rejoice over me,
> who boast against me when my foot slips!"
> For I am ready to fall, and my pain is ever before me.
> I confess my iniquity; I am sorry for my sin.
> But my foes are vigorous, they are mighty,
> and many are those who hate me wrongfully.
> Those who render me evil for good
> accuse me because I follow after good.
> Do not forsake me, O Lord!
> O my God, be not far from me!
> Make haste to help me, O Lord, my salvation!
> Psalm 38

Trouble in this world

In John 16:33 Jesus states that we will have trouble in this world. It is a fact of life and we should get used to it. We need encouragement to help us to deal with this world. Encouragement makes it easier to live in this fallen world. And Jesus here gives us a word of encouragement, that he has overcome the world and by inference, we have overcome the world also as we abide in Him.

> I have said these things to you,
> that in me you may have peace.
> In the world you will have tribulation.
> But take heart; I have overcome the world."
> John 16:33

Encouragement gives us hope

One reason to read the Old Testament is that it was written for our instruction. The encouragement of the Scriptures gives us hope.

> For whatever was written in former days was written for our instruction, that through endurance and through the encouragement of the Scriptures we might have hope.
> Romans 15:4

Encouragement helps in hard times

> And have you forgotten the exhortation that addresses you as sons?
> "My son, do not regard lightly the discipline of the Lord,
> nor be weary when reproved by him.
> For the Lord disciplines the one he loves,
> and chastises every son whom he receives."
> Hebrews 12:5,6

Being disciplined by the Lord proves His love for us. What we may think is tough discipline is actually a blessing.

Chapter 4 Where Do We Get Encouragement?

From the Scriptures

We get our encouragement from many different sources: from Church, friends, books, articles, favorite activities, etc. But ultimately, we need to get our encouragement from the Scriptures. Much of the Psalms, as well as many of the letters in the New Testament, are full of encouragement. You cannot help but trip over passages on encouragement.

Romans 15 points us back to the scriptures for encouragement:

> For everything that was written
> in the past was written to teach us,
> so that through the endurance taught in the
> Scriptures and the encouragement
> they provide we might have hope.
> Romans 15:1-7

Do not lose heart

Here we have strong encouragement despite growing older with (light and momentary) afflictions. We are to look beyond the things that we can see in the here and now and look at the things that we see with eyes of faith.

So, we do not lose heart. Though our outer self is wasting away, our inner self is being renewed day by day. For this light momentary affliction is preparing for us an eternal weight of glory beyond all comparison, as we look not to the things that are seen but to the things that are unseen. For the things that are seen are transient, but the things that are unseen are eternal.
II Corinthians 4:16-18

Some questions to consider

Philippians 2:3,4 says *"Do nothing from selfish ambition or conceit but in humility count others more significant than yourselves. Let each of you look not only to his own interests but also to the interests of others."*

- How is doing nothing from selfish ambition or conceit contribute to encouragement?
- How is counting others as more significant than ourselves part of encouragement?
- How should we view others while encouraging them?
- Why is humility so important in viewing others?
- How do you discover another person's interest?
- How does counting others more significant than ourselves encourage them?

Chapter 5 Prayers for the Encourager

In addition to verbal and written encouragement, the encourager should be praying to encourage others.

Following are just a few examples of prayers to encourage someone. There are many more that can be found in Scripture. You could also make up your own prayers. The following may give you some ideas.

That Christ may dwell in your hearts

For this reason I bow my knees before the Father, from whom every family in heaven and on earth is named, that according to the riches of his glory he may grant you to be strengthened with power through his Spirit in your inner being, so that Christ may dwell in your hearts through faith— that you, being rooted and grounded in love, may have strength to comprehend with all the saints what is the breadth and length and height and depth, and to know the love of Christ that surpasses knowledge, that you may be filled with all the fullness of God. – Ephesians 3:14-19

Be renewed in the spirit of your minds

. . . and be renewed in the spirit of your minds, and to put on the new self, created after the likeness of God in true righteousness and holiness. Ephesians 4:23,24

Walk in a manner worthy of your calling

I, therefore, a prisoner for the Lord, urge you to walk in a manner worthy of the calling to which you have been called, with all humility and gentleness, with patience, bearing with one another in love, eager to maintain the unity of the Spirit in the bond of peace. There is one body and one Spirit—just as you were called to the one hope that belongs to your call—one Lord, one faith, one baptism, one God and Father of all, who is over all and through all and in all. But grace was given to each one of us according to the measure of Christ's gift. Ephesians 4:1-7

Rejoice in hope and be patient in tribulation

That you would rejoice in hope and be patient in tribulation. – Romans 12:12

Live in harmony with one another

May the God of endurance and encouragement grant you to live in such harmony with one another, in accordance with Christ Jesus, that together you may with one voice glorify the God and Father of our Lord Jesus Christ. Romans 15:5-6

May God comfort your hearts

Now may our Lord Jesus Christ himself, and God our Father, who loved us and gave us eternal comfort and good hope through grace, comfort your hearts and establish them in every good work and word. II Thessalonians 2:16-17

Walk according to His commandments

And this is love, that we walk according to his commandments; this is the commandment, just as you have heard from the beginning so that you should walk in it. II John 1:6

Filled with the knowledge of His will

And so, from the day we heard, we have not ceased to pray for you, asking that you may be filled with the knowledge of his will in all spiritual wisdom and understanding, so as to walk in a manner worthy of the Lord, fully pleasing to him: bearing fruit in every good work and increasing in the knowledge of God; being strengthened with all power, according to his glorious might, for all endurance and patience with joy; giving thanks to the Father, who has qualified you to share in the inheritance of the saints in light. Colossians 1:9-12

Chapter 6 Strong and Courageous

Following are some examples from the scriptures on encouragement.

Moses encourages Joshua

Moses was commanded by God to encourage Joshua who would take over the responsibility of leading the Israelites. Although Joshua was Moses's second in command for years, learning about leading and leading are actually two different things. Here is what God told Moses to impart to Joshua:

> Joshua the son of Nun, who stands before you, he shall enter. Encourage him, for he shall cause Israel to inherit it. Deuteronomy 1:38

Be strong and courageous

In these verses, Joshua is receiving encouragement and promises as he is being prepared to be the next leader of Israel after Moses.

> Then Moses summoned Joshua and said to him in the
> sight of all Israel, "Be strong and courageous, for you
> shall go with this people into the land that
> the Lord has sworn to their fathers to give them, and
> you shall put them in possession of it. It is
> the Lord who goes before you. He will be with
> you; he will not leave you or forsake you. Do not fear
> or be dismayed."
> Deuteronomy 31:7-8

Our encouragement

And for us, Psalm 34 is our encouragement.

> Oh, taste and see that the Lord is good!
> Blessed is the man who takes refuge in him!
> Oh, fear the Lord, you his saints,
> for those who fear him have no lack!
> Psalm 34:8-9

Continuing on in Psalm 121:

> I lift up my eyes to the hills.
> From where does my help come?
> My help comes from the Lord,
> who made heaven and earth.
> He will not let your foot be moved;
> he who keeps you will not slumber.
> Behold, he who keeps Israel
> will neither slumber nor sleep.
> The Lord is your keeper;
> the Lord is your shade on your right hand.
> The sun shall not strike you by day,
> nor the moon by night.
> The Lord will keep you from all evil;
> he will keep your life.
> The Lord will keep
> your going out and your coming in
> from this time forth and forevermore.
> Psalm 121:1-8

The Name of the Lord – a Strong Tower

Here in Proverbs the Name of the Lord is described as a strong tower and says the righteous man runs into it to be safe. Don't we do the same thing? When we get into trouble for whatever reason, we may retreat either mentally or go to a place of safety that we associate with the Lord. But the Lord is with us whenever and wherever we go.

> The name of the Lord is a strong tower;
> the righteous man runs into it and is safe.
> Proverbs 18:10

Chapter 7 Biblical Promises & Narratives

Much encouragement may be gleaned by looking at Biblical promises or narratives.

Following are examples of just a few.

David and Jonathan

The story of David and Jonathan is epic.

David was the youngest son of Jesse (grandson of Boaz and Ruth). David is the one who slays the giant Philistine Goliath at the Valley of Elah. It is the Valley of Elah where the Philistine army is fighting Saul's army. Saul is the King of Israel and the father of Jonathan.

David's victory against Goliath encouraged Israel's army to rout the Philistines and drive them back to Gath and the gates of Ekron. After the battle, Abner was sent by Saul to find out who David was. When David was brought before Saul, "And Saul said to him, 'Whose son are you, young man?' And David answered, 'I am the son of your servant Jesse the Bethlehemite.' "

Jonathan who is the eldest son of Saul had also been fighting the Philistines. Jonathan takes an immediate liking to David and the two form a covenant.

The covenant between David and Jonathan

> As soon as he had finished speaking to Saul, the soul of Jonathan was knit to the soul of David, and Jonathan loved him as his own soul. And Saul took him that day and would not let him return to his father's house. Then Jonathan made a covenant with David, because he loved him as his own soul. And Jonathan stripped himself of the robe that was on him and gave it to David, and his armor, and even his sword and his bow and his belt. And David went out and was successful wherever Saul sent him, so that Saul set him over the men of war. And this was good in the sight of all the people and also in the sight of Saul's servants. I Samuel 18:1-5

As time went on Saul began to hate David because the people praised David over Saul. There was an incident where Saul, being filled with a harmful spirit, hurled a spear at David. The Lord had rejected Saul and chosen in his stead David as King of Israel.

David and Jonathan's friendship

Encouragement as seen through the friendship of David and Jonathan.

> David saw that Saul had come out to seek his life. David was in the wilderness of Ziph at Horesh. And Jonathan, Saul's son, rose and went to David at Horesh, and strengthened his hand in God. And he said to him, "Do not fear, for the hand of Saul my father shall not find you. You shall be king over Israel, and I shall be next to you. Saul my father also knows this." And the two of them made a covenant before the Lord. David remained at Horesh, and Jonathan went home. I Samuel 23:15-18

On the road to Emmaus

In Luke 24:13-32 we find two disciples walking on the road to Emmaus a few days after the crucifixion of Jesus. Jesus joins them but keeps his identity hidden. He encourages the two by just listening for a while and then opens the scriptures.

Here is the passage for the road to Emmaus.

That very day two of them were going to a village named Emmaus, about seven miles from Jerusalem, and they were talking with each other about all these things that had happened. While they were talking and discussing together, Jesus himself drew near and went with them. But their eyes were kept from recognizing him. And he said to them, "What is this conversation that you are holding with each other as you walk?" And they stood still, looking sad. Then one of them, named Cleopas, answered him, "Are you the only visitor to Jerusalem who does not know the things that have happened there in these days?" And he said to them, "What things?" And they said to him, "Concerning Jesus of Nazareth, a man who was a prophet mighty in deed and word before God and all the people, and how our chief priests and rulers delivered him up to be condemned to death, and crucified him. But we had hoped that he was the one to redeem Israel.

Yes, and besides all this, it is now the third day since these things happened. Moreover, some women of our company amazed us. They were at the tomb early in the morning, and when they did not find his body, they came back saying that they had even seen a vision of angels, who said that he was alive. Some of those who were with us went to the tomb and found it just as the women had said, but him they did not see." And he said to them, "O foolish ones, and slow of heart to believe all that the prophets have spoken!

Was it not necessary that the Christ should suffer these things and enter into his glory?" And beginning with Moses and all the Prophets, he interpreted to them in all the Scriptures the things concerning himself
So they drew near to the village to which they were going. He acted as if he were going farther, but they urged him strongly, saying, "Stay with us, for it is toward evening and the day is now far spent." So he went in to stay with them. When he was at table with them, he took the bread and blessed and broke it and gave it to them. And their eyes were opened, and they recognized him. And he vanished from their sight. They said to each other, **"Did not our hearts burn within us while he talked to us on the road, while he opened to us the Scriptures?"**
Luke 24:13-32

Please notice verse 32, the last sentence, "Did not our hearts burn within us while he talked to us on the road, while he opened to us the Scriptures?" This is this is a good prayer for yourself and others, that our hearts will burn as we look into the Scriptures.

The example of Barnabas

One of the best examples in the Scriptures of an encourager is Barnabas. Barnabas's real name was Joseph; he was a Levite who lived in Cyprus. In fact, the name Barnabas actually means "son of encouragement." Acts 4:36

After Paul's conversion, he tried to get with the other disciples, but they were afraid of him (remember his past of persecuting Christians see Acts 8:1-3). So, it was up to Barnabas to bring Paul to the Apostles and explain to them that Paul was indeed a disciple now:

And when he had come to Jerusalem, he attempted to join the disciples. And they were all afraid of him, for they did not believe that he was a disciple. But Barnabas took him and brought him to the apostles and declared to them how on the road he had seen the Lord, who spoke to him, and how at Damascus he had preached boldly in the name of Jesus. So he went in and out among them at Jerusalem, preaching boldly in the name of the Lord. Acts 9:26-28

It is said of Barnabas:

for he was a good man,
full of the Holy Spirit and of faith.
Acts 11:24

See verses Acts 11:23-26, Acts 13:43, Acts 14:21-23, Acts 15:32-35 for more information regarding Barnabas.

Jesus has us securely in his care

> My sheep hear my voice, and I know them, and they
> follow me. I give them eternal life, and they will never
> perish, and no one will snatch them out of my hand.
> My Father, who has given them to me, is greater than
> all, and no one is able to snatch them out of the
> Father's hand. I and the Father are one."
> John 10:27-30

Here Jesus is talking about his sheep, and how his
sheep know his voice and follow him. He also gives
his sheep (us) eternal life and we will never perish.
Then he refers to his Father, and the security we have
in God.

Encouragement for our walk

> And we know that for those who love God all things
> work together for good· for those who are called
> according to his purpose. For those whom
> he foreknew he also predestined to be conformed to
> the image of his Son, in order that he might be the
> firstborn among many brothers. And those whom he
> predestined he also called, and those whom he called
> he also justified, and those whom he justified he
> also glorified.
> Romans 8:28-30

- Encouragement in all things working together for
good. We are called according to his purpose.

- Encouragement that God foreknew and predestined us to be conformed to his image.

- Encouragement in that those whom he predestined, he also called, then justified and then glorified.

Escaping temptation

There is encouragement here, in that with the temptation God will <u>always</u> provide a way to escape it.

> No temptation has overtaken you that is not common to man. God is faithful, and he will not let you be tempted beyond your ability, but with the temptation he will also provide the way of escape, that you may be able to endure it.
> I Corinthians 10:13

God's everlasting love

What then shall we say to these things? If God is for us, who can be against us? He who did not spare his own Son but gave him up for us all, how will he not also with him graciously give us all things? Who shall bring any charge against God's elect? It is God who justifies. Who is to condemn? Christ Jesus is the one who died—more than that, who was raised—who is at the right hand of God, who indeed is interceding for us. Who shall separate us from the love of Christ? Shall tribulation, or distress, or persecution, or famine, or nakedness, or danger, or sword? As it is written,

"For your sake we are being killed all the day long; we are regarded as sheep to be slaughtered."

No, in all these things we are more than conquerors through him who loved us. For I am sure that neither death nor life, nor angels nor rulers, nor things present nor things to come, nor powers, nor height nor depth, nor anything else in all creation, will be able to separate us from the love of God in Christ Jesus our Lord.
Romans 8:31-39

This is a pinnacle of God's love for the elect.

From the previous passage:

- If God is for us, what can possibly be against us?

- Since God did not spare His Son, he will give us all things.

- How can the elect be charged with anything, God is the judge.

- We cannot be condemned, Christ died for us.

- Nothing separates us from the love of God, not tribulation, distress, persecution, famine, nakedness, danger, or the sword.

- We are more than conquerors through Christ who loves us.

- And again, a list of things that cannot separate us from God: death nor life, nor angels nor rulers, nor things present nor things to come, nor powers, nor height nor depth, nor anything else in all creation, will be able to separate us from the love of God in Christ Jesus our Lord.

Amen and Amen!

Not forsaken

> The Lord is a stronghold for the oppressed,
> a stronghold in times of trouble.
> And those who know your name put their trust in you,
> for you, O Lord, have not forsaken those who seek you.
> Psalms 9:9,10

This is a real encouragement, that those who seek the Lord will not be forsaken.

End of the world promises

These are the end of the world promises. I know we have to wait but still, it is hard. No more pain, or mourning! It is such an encouragement just to read this verse.

> He will wipe away every tear from their eyes, and death shall be no more, neither shall there be mourning, nor crying, nor pain anymore, for the former things have passed away."
> Revelation 21:4

One final note

The happiest Christians are those who have found the joy of encouraging others. The quickest way to end a own pity party is to find someone whom you can encourage.

Other books by Mike Kadow

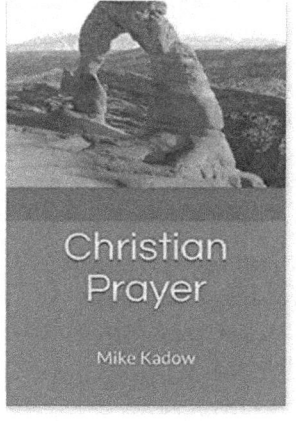

This book covers the basics of prayer. It starts with the question of "How can a Christian Pray to a Holy, Perfect and Preeminent God?" Then it goes on to talk about some of the necessary elements of prayer, like:

- Hunger for God, God's Spirit
- Faith,   Praise and Worship
- Thanksgiving,
- Confession and Repentance
- Praying for oneself and others,
- Praying for the lost

It then goes into:

- Creating your own unique Prayer Life
- Praying the Scriptures
- Phrases that address and describe God
- Faith and God's Attributes

    God's attributes are briefly described to give the reader a better idea of the God to whom we are praying. A good understanding of God is essential to an effective prayer life.

Other subjects in Prayer, where do we go from here?

Other Books by Mike Kadow

The woman said to the snake, "We may eat the fruit of the garden's trees but not the fruit of the tree in the middle of the garden. God said, 'Don't eat from it, and don't touch it, or you will die.'" Genesis 3:2-3

Perhaps if Adam and Eve were more thankful for what they already had, and not looking for what they thought they wanted, things would be different.

The same is true with us, we are admonished to count our blessings because we tend to forget what we already have.

"Thank you," we say it every day. And many times in a day. But why? We were told by our parents it is the polite thing to say. "Please and thank you." And then we drill it into our own children. In American society "please and thank you" go a long way. We are told, it is only being polite.

Being polite, yes, but in the Bible, it goes much deeper than that. We shall see that saying "Thank You" and having a constant attitude of thankfulness and gratitude is actually a form of godliness. Or if it is not a form of godliness, it goes a long way to keep us out of sin. How does it do that you might ask. If you are more concerned with being polite and gracious, saying please and thank you and having an attitude of gratefulness as the Bible encourages us, you have less time to be thinking of the evil you might otherwise be doing. That is the "how."

My Testimony

As a Christian, I would be remiss if I did not express the tenets of my belief:

- Sola Fide, by faith alone.

- Sola Scriptura, by Scripture alone.

- Solus Christus, through Christ alone.

- Sola Gratia, by grace alone.

- Soli Deo Gloria, glory to God alone.

I joined the US Army in July of 1968. During Basic Training I was reading from *Good News for Modern Man*, a New Testament translation someone had given to me. I was reading the passages about many are called but few are chosen. Matthew 22:14

Then one Sunday afternoon word came down regarding some event on the Parade Grounds. We were told it was not mandatory but "you will be there!" When we were all gathered someone was talking to us about Jesus Christ. An invitation was given, and I found myself going forward.

A week or so later I had a meeting with a Chaplain Johnson. He kept stressing this verse in the Bible, Revelation 3:20, "Behold, I stand at the door and knock. If anyone hears my voice and opens the door, I will come to him and eat with him, and he with me." I was not sure what the Chaplain was talking about, nor what Jesus was talking about in the verse. But whatever it was, I wanted it. Several nights later, I invited Jesus into my life.

A few weeks later, I arrived at my next duty station; it was the Naval School of Music in Norfolk Virginia, and I was preparing for the US Army Band. I knew I was a Christian, not sure how I knew but I did. I also knew that Christians attend Bible Studies. So I found a Bible Study listed on the bulletin board. I went to the Study and it was there I met Fred (not his real name). Fred was a chief in the Navy. Fred took an interest in me and invited me to his home for the weekend. I had no other offers, being 3000 miles away from home, so I accepted. I remember on the drive to his house he kept asking me questions about my choosing Christ.

The next morning Fred had somewhere to go so he sat me down and had me listen to a tape on Scripture Memory. And with that word of guidance, I started my Christian life.

If you have never considered what it means to be a Christian, there is no time like the present. You could die tonight in your sleep and find yourself standing before the God of all creation. If you feel Christ tugging at your heart, repent of your sins and turn to God and never look back.

Revelation 3:20 "Behold, I stand at the door and knock. If anyone hears my voice and opens the door, I will come into him and eat with him, and he with me."

Amen and Amen.

Printed in the USA
CPSIA information can be obtained
at www.ICGtesting.com
LVHW042242150124
768989LV00037B/593

9 781724 026903